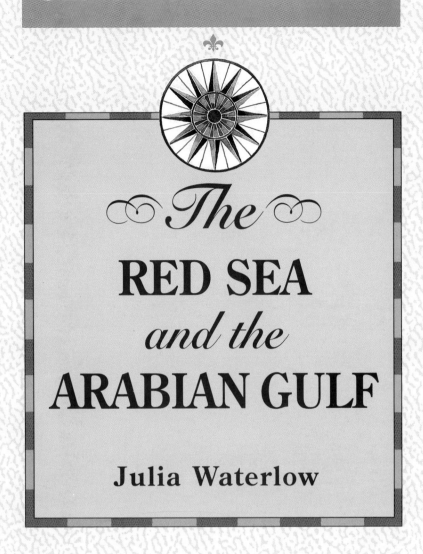

The
RED SEA
and the
ARABIAN GULF

Julia Waterlow

WAYLAND

Seas and Oceans series

The Atlantic Ocean
The Caribbean and the Gulf of Mexico
The Indian Ocean
The Mediterranean Sea
The North Sea and the Baltic Sea
The Pacific Ocean
The Polar Seas
The Red Sea and the Arabian Gulf

Cover: A coral reef in the Red Sea.

Series and book editor: Katie Orchard
Series designer: Stonecastle Graphics Ltd
Production controller: Caroline Davis

First published in 1996 by
Wayland Publishers Limited
61 Western Road, Hove
East Sussex BN3 1JD, England

© Copyright 1996 Wayland Publishers Limited

British Library Cataloguing in Publication Data
Waterlow, Julia
  The Red Sea and the Arabian Gulf. – (Seas and Oceans series)
  1. Red Sea – Juvenile literature
  2. Persian Gulf – Juvenile literature
  I. Title
910'.0216533

ISBN 0 7502 1742 1

Printed and bound by L.E.G.O. S.p.A., Vicenza, Italy.

Picture acknowledgements:
Dieter Betz 12, 15, 27 (bottom), 36, 45;
James Davis Travel Photography 9, 14, 16,
29 (right), 33 (top); Ecoscene 18, (Mark
Caney), 20 (top right/Mark Caney), 34
(Adrian Morgan); Eye Ubiquitous 5
(Christopher Portway), 13 (Paul Dowd), 20
(bottom left), 37 (Paul Dowd), 40 (Paul
Dowd), 41 (Julia Waterlow); Impact 28–9
(top/Alan Keohane), 38 (John Norman), 39
(Caroline Penn), 44 (top right/ Schurr/
Cedri); Frank Lane Picture Agency 19 (Ian
Cartwright), 21 (Ian Cartwright), 24 (R.
Commer/Earthviews), 25 (E&D Hosking),
41 (A. Parker); Oxford Scientific Films 23
(David Fleetham); Panos Pictures 31 (Guy
Mansfield), 32 (Alain le Garsmeur); Planet
Earth Pictures 22 (Georgette Douwma);
Science Photo Library 11 (NASA); Tony
Stone Worldwide 26 (Nabeel Turner), 27
(top), 42 (Chris Haigh), 43 (Jeff Rotman), 44
(bottom left); Julia Waterlow 7, 28 (bottom),
30; Zefa cover (Tekano).
All artwork is produced by Hardlines except
Peter Bull 33 (bottom).

Contents

Words that appear in **bold** in the text can be found in the glossary on page 46.

INTRODUCTION
The Desert Seas

The Red Sea and Arabian Gulf are like a finger and thumb of water, pointing up from the vast Indian Ocean into the part of the world known as the Middle East. To the east is the **continent** of Asia, to the west, Africa, and to the north, Europe. The Red Sea and Arabian Gulf lie on the cross-roads between these continents.

The two seas are almost entirely surrounded by land, but they have narrow channels at the southern end joining them with the Indian Ocean. Between the seas is a block of land known as the Arabian **Peninsula**. The shimmering greens and blues of the water contrast with the sun-scorched yellows and browns of the coasts, since much of the land around is barren desert.

The Red Sea and the Arabian Gulf lie in the Middle East. The Arabian Gulf is also sometimes known as the Persian Gulf and is often shortened to 'the Gulf'.

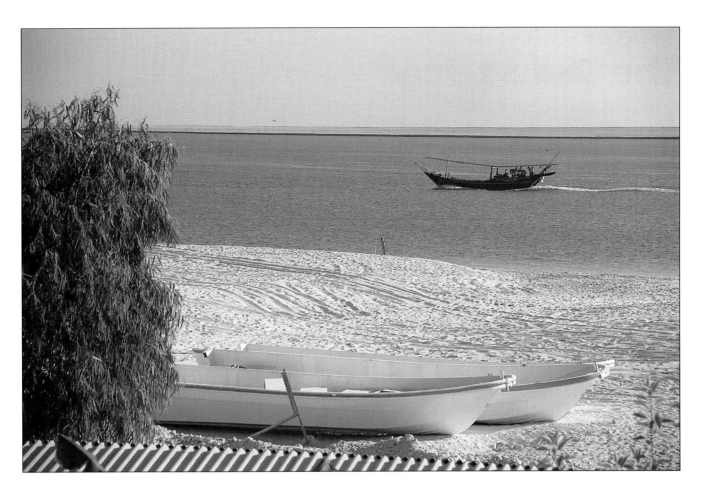

The deserts and lack of water mean that the land is sparsely populated. Saudi Arabia, for example, has an area ten times that of Britain, yet its population is only a quarter of the size. There are only a few settlements on the Red Sea coasts, but in the Arabian Gulf there are new ports and modern cities which were built when oil was discovered in the area. Not long ago, the people of the Arabian Gulf lived simple **subsistence** lives. Now the countries around the Arabian Gulf are among the world's richest because oil has brought great wealth to this area. In contrast, neighbouring countries that do not have oil are much poorer.

The Red Sea and Arabian Gulf are relatively small compared with the great oceans. Even so, they are important seas. The Arabian Gulf has the largest **oil reserves** in the world and fleets of oil **tankers** sail across its waters. Although the Red Sea has not been developed in the same way as the Arabian Gulf, it is a vital international waterway linking the Mediterranean Sea with the Indian Ocean via the Suez Canal. The Red Sea also has a very special natural feature – some of the longest and most unspoilt coral reefs in world.

At Abu Dhabi, on the Arabian Gulf, a boat leaves port to go fishing in the shallow waters along the sandy desert coasts.

The Red Sea

The Red Sea is long and thin, running almost north to south. It separates the shores of Africa and Arabia – on the west side lie Egypt, Sudan and Ethiopia, and on the east side lie Saudi Arabia and Yemen.

In the far north, the Red Sea divides into two narrow stretches of water: the Gulf of Suez and the Gulf of Aqaba, split by the Sinai Peninsula. A small neck of land divides the Gulf of Suez from the Mediterranean Sea, but the Suez Canal has been cut through the **isthmus** so that ships can travel from one sea to the other. The Red Sea narrows at its southern end and a **strait**, called the Bab al Mandab Strait, connects the Red Sea with the Gulf of Aden.

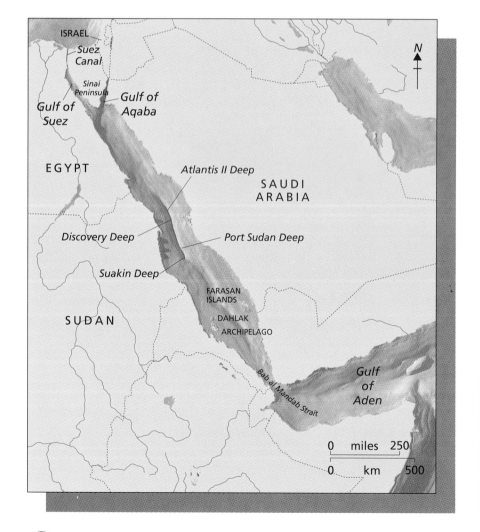

The Red Sea is like a long, thin trench filled with water. Although shallow around the edge, it plunges deep down in the middle.

The size of the Red Sea
Area: 438,000 km²
Length: 1,930 km
Maximum width: 306 km
Maximum depth: 2,920 m

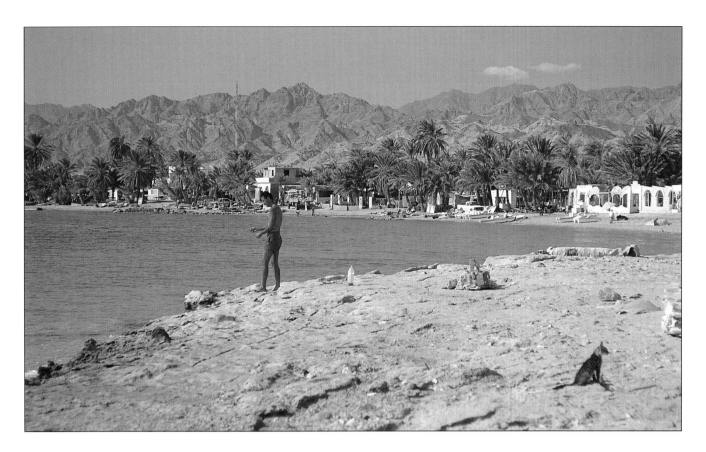

Although the Red Sea is shallow near the coasts, it drops down to great depths in the middle. Running along the centre of the Red Sea is a deep trough, or underwater valley, which in places is very rugged. Here, several sharp clefts, like deep pits, appear in the sea-bed and plunge down 2,900 m below sea-level.

This tourist village lies on the coast of the mountainous Sinai Peninsula which divides the Gulf of Aqaba from the Gulf of Suez at the northern end of the Red Sea.

Among the special features of the Red Sea are its coral reefs. The reefs mostly occur near the coasts in shallower waters and stretch for thousands of kilometres around the edges of the sea. In places, the coral has grown across harbours, such as at Suakin in Sudan. In the southern part of the Red Sea, the coral growth has left only narrow channels that ships can sail through and, at the Bab al Mandab Strait, the coral has to be blasted and **dredged** so that ships can pass through. Over the centuries, many ships have been wrecked on the Red Sea coral reefs, and treasure hunters still find ships that sank over 2,000 years ago.

There are islands dotted around the Red Sea, but they are nearly all uninhabited. Many are exposed coral reefs with just sand or a few bushes, but near the Dahlak Archipelago is a group of active volcanoes.

The Arabian Gulf

The Arabian Gulf is about half the size of the Red Sea and is shorter and wider. Like the Red Sea, it is **landlocked** at its northern end and a narrow channel, called the Strait of Hormuz, joins it to the Gulf of Oman and the Indian Ocean. Lying to the west is the Arabian Peninsula, and to the east lies Iran.

The Arabian Gulf is a very shallow sea; in places it is no deeper than 90 m. The sea-bed slopes gently down from west to east, with the deepest water along the coast of Iran where the rugged Zagros Mountains come down to the sea. The Arabian coast is low-lying and fringed by sandy beaches, mudflats and **lagoons**. Sandy islands, such as Bahrain, lie offshore. Around the narrow Strait of Hormuz, cliffs plunge into the sea, and the rocky coast and small islands make it a dangerous area for shipping.

On the Arabian side, the Gulf is shallow with sandy islands and lagoons; on the Iranian side, the water is deeper and the coast is much rockier.

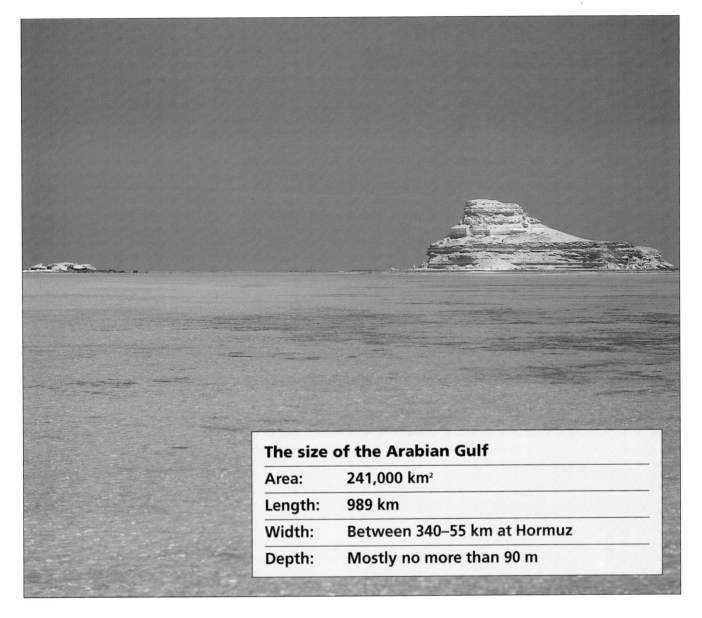

The size of the Arabian Gulf	
Area:	241,000 km²
Length:	989 km
Width:	Between 340–55 km at Hormuz
Depth:	Mostly no more than 90 m

At the northern end of the Gulf, there is a wide plain where three rivers, the Tigris, Euphrates and Karun, flow out into the sea. Over thousands of years, these rivers have brought huge amounts of **sediment** downstream. The sediment has been dropped as the rivers slowed down and reached the sea, and created a low-lying marshy **delta**.

The Arabian Gulf may have once been part of a much larger, deeper basin, which has gradually been filled by sediment. Some sediment would have been blown from the land or carried down by rivers, and some would be the remains of dead sea creatures. The thick layers of sediment (hundreds of metres deep) have left the surface of the sea floor very smooth. Oil and gas have formed in these sediments.

Much of the Gulf has shallow, clear water such as here off the coast of Abu Dhabi.

The Moving Earth

The Red Sea lies in a gap between Africa and Arabia, where the Earth is being pulled apart. The surface of the Earth is made up of pieces of hard crust, known as plates. These float like skin on molten rock that lies deep down in the Earth, where it is very hot. Driven by the heat below, the plates slowly move around, sometimes colliding with each other and sometimes splitting apart. They usually move at a rate of a few centimetres a year.

Geologists think that Africa and Arabia started moving away from each other about 30 million years ago, although the most northern and southern parts of the Red Sea may have only opened up about 4 million years ago. The trough that appeared filled with sea water from the Indian Ocean.

The crust of the Earth is broken up into plates which slowly move around, splitting apart and colliding. This map shows what is happening in the Middle East and East Africa.

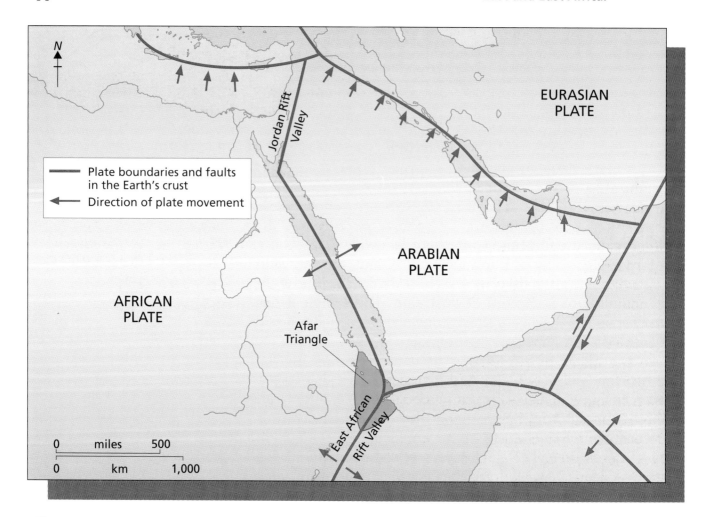

N

EURASIAN PLATE

Jordan Rift Valley

— Plate boundaries and faults in the Earth's crust

← Direction of plate movement

ARABIAN PLATE

AFRICAN PLATE

Afar Triangle

East African Rift Valley

0   miles   500
0   km   1,000

Part of the Afar Triangle in Djibouti as seen from a satellite. The inlet of water at the bottom right is part of the Gulf of Aden. The red landscape is mostly bleak and desolate rock. The black patches are lava (molten volcanic rock) flows and the white areas are salt lakes.

The Red Sea is a relatively new sea in terms of the **geological history** of the Earth, and it is growing. If the African and Arabian plates continue to spread apart at their present rate, in 200 million years, the Red Sea will become as wide as the Atlantic Ocean.

The trough filled by the waters of the Red Sea is part of a long system of cracks in the Earth's crust, caused by the stresses and strains of plate movements in this region. The East African Rift Valley continues south for about another 3,500 km and the Dead Sea-Jordan Rift Valley is a trough that carries on north from the Gulf of Aqaba.

The Afar Triangle

The Afar Triangle is a flat triangle of land on the African side of the Red Sea. It lies at the very southern end of the Red Sea, where it meets the Gulf of Aden and the East African Rift Valley, and is part of the trough caused by the spreading continents.

The Afar Triangle was once covered by the sea, but earth movements lifted the land up above sea-level. It is an area of inhospitable desert covered in thick layers of salt left by the sea and the remains of old volcanoes.

In contrast to the Red Sea, the Arabian Gulf lies where two plates of the Earth's crust are colliding. As the Red Sea has split apart, the Arabian plate has been pushed eastwards and collided with the much larger Eurasian plate. The Arabian plate has buckled and been pushed downwards at its eastern edge along the coast of Iran. This is why the sea-bed slopes down to the east and the water is deeper here. Pressure on the Eurasian plate has caused it to crumple and created the mountains behind the Iranian coast.

Cloudless Skies

The Red Sea and Arabian Gulf lie in one of the hottest, driest parts of the world. Daytime temperatures in summer can be over 40 °C, and in winter are rarely less than 20 °C. The north is usually a little cooler than the south: winter temperatures in Kuwait have been known to fall as low as 3 °C.

What little rain there is usually falls as short, heavy showers in the winter months of January and February. In the Gulf state of Bahrain, for example, it only rains on ten days a year on average, and the total rainfall in most of the area is under 100 mm a year. Tropical storms are rare, although in winter there are sometimes sudden **squalls**, which cause waves big enough to sink small ships.

There is a stiff breeze blowing across the Red Sea. Although this helps local fishermen with their sailing boats, it can also make the water quite choppy.

A sandstorm in the deserts of the Arabian Peninsula. Winds can bring dust and sand swirling down to the sea.

Most of the land around the two seas is desert, which reaches right down to the edge of the seas. There are no lakes and few rivers. The only rivers in the area are the Tigris, Euphrates and Karun, and the River Nile which lies east of the Red Sea and flows north into the Mediterranean Sea.

The climate is hot and sticky, mainly because of the very high humidity (the dampness in the air) by the sea and the high temperatures. There are few clouds to keep the sun off and the air feels sticky and quite stifling at times. The intense heat causes a shimmering haze over the water and land, making it difficult to see very far.

Both the Red Sea and the Gulf have persistent **seasonal** winds, although they are rarely strong enough to cause very dangerous seas. The winds often bring clouds of sand and dust from the deserts, sometimes completely blotting out the sun. Winds in the Red Sea are mostly northerly, but during winter, strong westerlies blow up (called the Egyptian winds), bringing fog as well as sand. The most common wind in the Gulf is the shamal, which blows from the north mainly during summer.

Desert rivers

The Tigris and Euphrates rivers, which flow through the deserts of Iraq, are fed by rain and melted snow in mountains to the far north. The river valleys provide fertile and well-watered land for farming in an area with extremely low rainfall. Before reaching the Gulf, the rivers wind through lakes and marshes and finally join to become one channel, called the Shatt al Arab, which flows out into the sea. The rivers used to flood in spring and bring tonnes of sediment down to the Arabian Gulf, but now river flow is controlled by dams. More than 90 per cent of the rivers' water never reaches the Gulf – it either **evaporates** in the hot sun or is drawn off and used for watering crops.

Salty Seas

Both the Red Sea and Arabian Gulf are very salty seas. The amount of salt in sea water is referred to as salinity, and is measured in parts per thousand. The average sea-water salinity in the world is about 35 parts of salt to every 1,000 parts of water. Both the Red Sea and the Gulf have considerably higher salinities.

Most seas are filled by fresh water from rivers, which makes them less salty. But very little fresh water enters either the Red Sea or Arabian Gulf. Also, the hot sun causes huge amounts of sea water to evaporate (over 2,000 mm a year). Salt does not evaporate with the water but remains in the sea, so the water that is left becomes even saltier. The Gulf's salinity is higher than that of the Red Sea because it is shallower.

Salinity (Parts per thousand)	
Red Sea	
Average salinity	36
Gulf of Suez	40
Deep clefts	257
Arabian Gulf	
Average salinity	40
Arabian coast	60

Coastal saltflats (called sebkhas), *along the Gulf coast in the United Arab Emirates. The Red Sea and the Arabian Gulf are some of the saltiest seas in the world.*

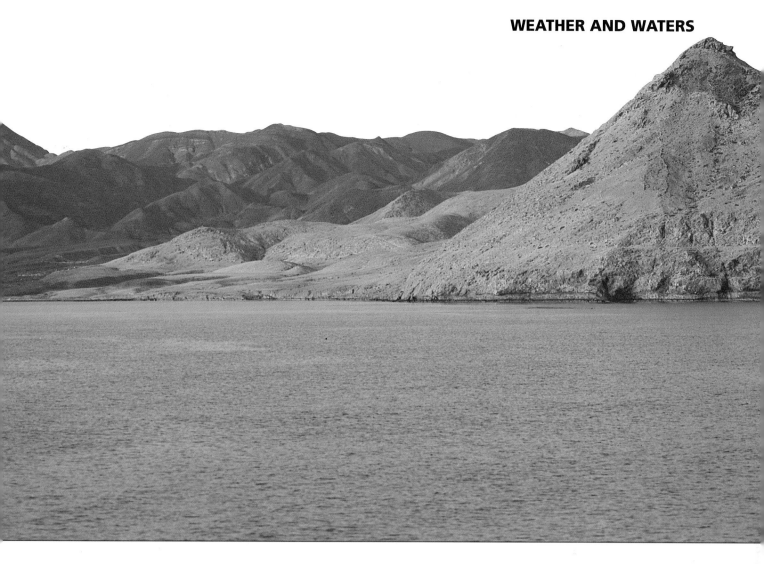

The narrow straits at the southern end of the seas mean that they are only slowly refilled by water from the Indian Ocean. If they were completely landlocked and not refilled by ocean water, they could dry out completely. It is thought that there have been times in the past when the Bab al Mandab Strait was blocked and the waters of the Red Sea evaporated, leaving a broad, salt-covered valley.

Dry deserts, such as this one in Egypt, surround the Red Sea on both sides and there are no permanent rivers to bring fresh water into the sea.

Surface water in both seas is very warm, but deeper down, the water is much cooler. Deeper water is also saltier, because salty water is heavier than fresh water, so it tends to sink. The deep clefts of the Red Sea have a peculiar feature. These clefts have pools of hot and very salty water, with temperatures as high as 100 °C and salinity five times higher than on the surface. Because the clefts lie in the middle of the sea, where the continental plates are pulling apart, it is thought that the heat and salt come from molten rock pushing up where the Earth's crust is thin.

Surface Temperatures	
Red Sea	up to 32 °C
Deep clefts	60–100 °C
Arabian Gulf	over 33 °C

Currents and Tides

Currents are strong movements of water in the sea that flow in one direction, rather like rivers. Surface currents in the Red Sea and Arabian Gulf are driven by winds that, in general, push water south during summer and north in winter. These currents are quite weak, except where the land narrows, such as at the Strait of Hormuz. Here, tidal water rushes through and, with the shifting and uncertain winds that blow around the cliffs, make it a difficult and dangerous passage of water to **navigate**.

Arab traders, such as these sailors in Dubai, have used the currents and winds of the Gulf for hundreds of years to sail these waters and reach far beyond.

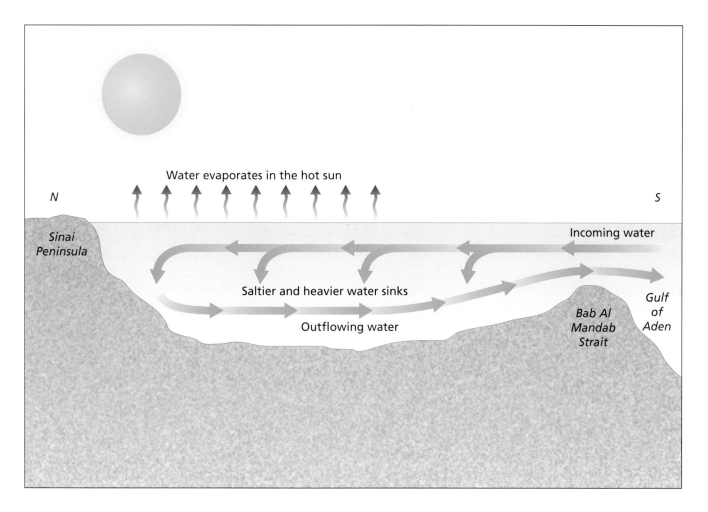

The strongest pattern of water circulation in the region is vertical, from the surface down to the depths. In the Red Sea, for example, water enters the region from the Indian Ocean through the Bab al Mandab Strait. As it warms up, the water begins to evaporate. It becomes saltier and heavier, and starts to sink. This heavier water flows south underneath the incoming water from the ocean. It is thought that it takes twenty years for the water in the Red Sea to be completely renewed. Water circulates in the Gulf in a similar way.

Tides are caused by the gravitational pull of the moon. The waters of the Red Sea and the Arabian Gulf rise and fall every day because tidal water from the Indian Ocean sweeps in and out through the narrow straits at the southern end of both seas. The **tidal range** is small, at most about 2 m, and the effects of the tides are only seen at northern and southern ends of the seas. Rather like water sloshed from one end of a bath to the other, water in the middle tends to stay fairly level, while at the ends it rises and falls. At Port Sudan on the Red Sea, for example, there is hardly any tidal effect at all.

One of the features of both the Red Sea and the Arabian Gulf is the way the water circulates vertically. Water entering the Red Sea from the Indian Ocean is driven northwards by winds. A lot of water evaporates, especially in the shallower parts of the sea such as the Gulf of Suez. This leaves saltier water, which sinks down and flows out under the lighter, incoming water.

Coral Reefs

Divers come from all over the world to explore the beautiful coral reefs set in the clear waters of the Red Sea. The reefs are like underwater walls and terraces, covered in colourful and strange-shaped corals, and teeming with fish and other sea creatures.

Coral is made up of hundreds of tiny living creatures, called coral polyps, which are joined together. Coral polyps are related to sea anemones: they are tube-shaped with a mouth at one end that is surrounded by tentacles. They feed off tiny animals that drift past.

The reef's variety

Coral comes in all sorts of shapes and colours, depending on water temperature, waves and the amount of light. Delicate branched, fan-shaped and soft corals grow in sheltered waters; hard, rounded 'brain' corals grow on the outside edge of the reef, where there are waves that would damage other kinds of coral; plate-like corals spread out in deeper waters to make a large surface area to catch as much light as possible. The Red Sea has more than 350 different types of coral.

A delicate fan coral spreads out from a reef in the Red Sea.

The coral reef drops down like a wall on the side facing the open sea. Colourful corals cluster on the side of the reef.

As the polyps grow, they make a hard, protective shell around their bodies which is cemented to other polyp shells. In this way, the reef builds up. The hard skeletons of dead corals make up most of the reef, but the surface is alive. Coral grows very slowly and it can take twenty years for a piece of coral to reach the size of a football. It will carry on growing outwards and upwards, but never above the surface of the water because the polyps cannot live in air.

Coral is very delicate and needs special conditions in order to grow. Coral likes warm water, preferably where the temperature is between 22–28 °C. Since reef-building coral needs sunlight to help it grow, it only lives in shallow water, usually no deeper than 30 m. For the same reason, coral needs clear water, without sediment or pollution, so it does not tend to thrive where rivers carry mud and **silt** down to the sea. There are fewer coral reefs in the Gulf, partly because of the warmer water and also because of sediments brought down by the Tigris and Euphrates rivers.

Fringing reefs lie parallel to the shores of the Red Sea and around some of the islands, and **barrier reefs**, are found further out to sea in slightly deeper waters. Inside the fringing reefs are shallow lagoons, but on the seaward side, the reefs slope steeply down.

Life on the Coral

The coral reefs are like tropical forests compared with the barren deserts surrounding the Red Sea. Thousands of different plants and creatures live there. Each living organism depends on another for food or shelter, and the reef supports a complex web of life, from tiny plants to big **predators**, such as sharks.

Some creatures attach themselves to coral, and wait for food to come to them. Sea anemones have tentacles to draw in small creatures that float within their grasp, while sponges and giant clams filter tiny pieces of plant food out of the water. There are other animals that move slowly over the coral, such as starfish, sea slugs and sea cucumbers. Sea urchins are very common, using their long, thin spines for defence and their teeth to scrape **algae** off the hard surface for food.

Shoals of brilliantly coloured and patterned fish swim in and out of the nooks and crevices in the coral. Many feed on algae such as seaweed, but others, such as wrasses, eat worms, shrimps and crabs. There are also predators, such as groupers, which eat smaller fish, and eels that use the coral

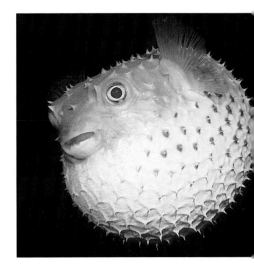

A pufferfish has blown itself up in a ball. It does this when threatened to make itself look more frightening.

The lionfish's striking markings act as a warning to predators; its deadly spines can inject poison into an attacker.

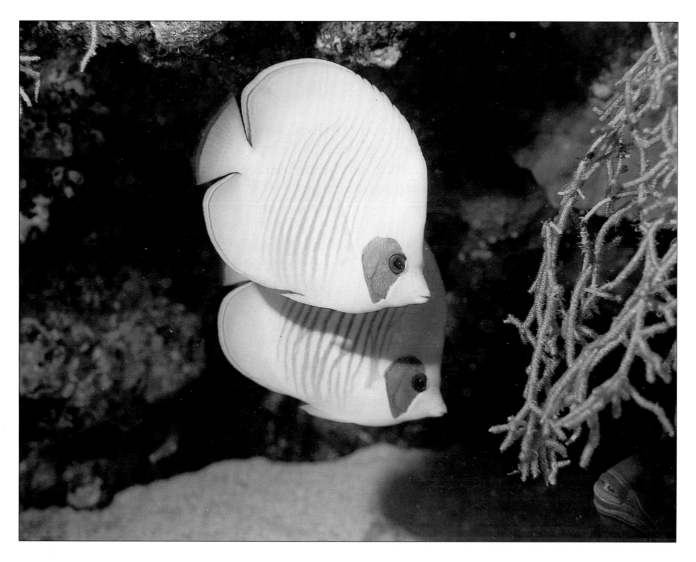

as hiding places to lurk in wait for their prey. Most life is found on the outside edge of the reef, and this suits predators, such as sharks, jacks, snappers and barracudas, which patrol the open waters in search of other fish to eat.

Angelfish, butterflyfish and damselfish are coloured in bright yellows, blues, greens and reds with stripes, patches and spots. The colours attract other fish of the same species, or warn predators that the fish is poisonous or unpleasant to eat.

Some creatures, such as the crown of thorns starfish and the parrot fish eat coral. In large numbers, these creatures can do great damage to coral reefs. However, the greatest threat can be from people. Pollution of the sea by waste materials from houses and factories can quickly kill coral. The coral reefs of the Red Sea are relatively unspoilt because so few people live along the shores.

Butterflyfish are some of the most brilliantly coloured fish of the reefs. They nearly always swim around in pairs like this.

Shallow Waters

Along the coasts of the Red Sea and Arabian Gulf are small inlets, where the water is shallow and fine mud and sands collect. Since they are rich in organic materials, the dense muds are short of oxygen, making it difficult for organisms to survive. Even so, plants and creatures have adapted to this **habitat**.

Mangrove trees grow in some of the inlets. Their roots stick up above the level of the mud so that the trees can get oxygen from the air. These aerial roots also help support the trees when swept by waves as the tide comes in. Few trees can tolerate salt water, but mangrove trees have a special way of getting rid of the salt through their leaves. The mangroves provide **nutrients** and shelter for many different fish and shellfish. Some shellfish, such as mussels, burrow in the mud leaving one end sticking out so that they can breathe. Crabs often burrow and wait for low tide before coming out to scavenge for food.

In the shallow waters of the Red Sea and the Gulf, there are beds of seagrass. This plant grows like a grass and provides a habitat where other plants and creatures, such as this long barbel goatfish and these wrasses, can thrive. This picture was taken in the Red Sea.

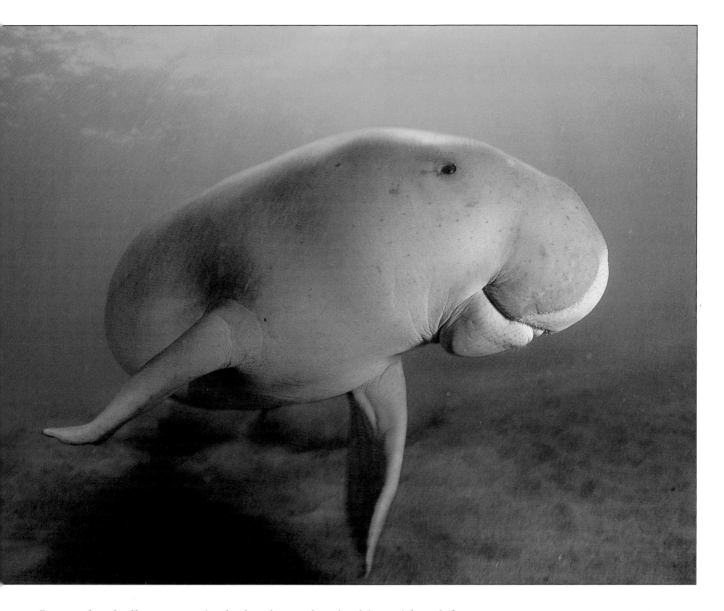

A dugong. These unusual creatures are mammals that graze on seagrass.

In sandy shallows, particularly along the Arabian side of the Gulf, there are large beds of seagrass. This is not a seaweed, but a true flowering plant with long, green leaves and spreading roots. Seagrasses provide shelter for small sea creatures, such as fish and shrimps, which eat tiny particles of plant and animal matter that collect on and among the seagrasses.

The largest creature that lives among the seagrass beds is the slow-moving dugong. This creature grazes on seagrass. Although they can live up to seventy years, dugongs breed very slowly. Dugongs are found in other parts of the world, but because they have been overhunted and their habitat destroyed, the number of dugongs is declining. There are about 12,000 dugongs left in the Red Sea and Arabian Gulf.

Other Plants and Creatures

One explanation for the name 'Red Sea' is that sometimes, large patches of a particular reddish-coloured phytoplankton are seen drifting on the sea's surface. Phytoplankton are microscopic plants that live off nutrients in the water. They need sunlight to survive, so they float near the surface. Phytoplankton are the basis of life in the sea. Corals, fish and other sea creatures feed on phytoplankton and in turn, these creatures provide food for others.

Since most phytoplankton is found near nutrient-rich coasts, these areas are also where the greatest number of other sea creatures are found. However, larger fish do cruise out in the

A diver swims with a whale shark. These gentle giants mainly feed off plankton.

Birds such as this sea eagle nest on islands in the Red Sea and Gulf. They survive by catching fish from the sea.

open waters of the Red Sea and the Gulf. The biggest of all are whale sharks, which are grey with white spots. Although they can grow up to 12 m long, whale sharks are harmless creatures and feed off tiny fish and plankton. Another large fish related to the shark is the manta ray, which can be up to 6 m wide. The manta ray is a flat fish with wings that flap slowly up and down as it moves through the water. Like the whale shark, the manta ray is a gentle creature and lives off plankton.

Death of the coral

Recently some large areas of coral died in the Red Sea. A thick mat of green algae had appeared, which smothered the coral and cut off its supply of food and light. A study carried out in Israel discovered that the massive growth was probably due to a volcanic eruption on the other side of the world. In 1991, Mount Pinatubo in the Philippines erupted, blasting dust into the atmosphere. The dust spread, filtered out the sun and caused low temperatures in several parts of the world. A very cold winter in the Middle East brought cool, nutrient-rich waters up to the surface of the Red Sea. The surge in nutrients caused the sudden algae growth.

The islands and shores around the Red Sea and Arabian Gulf are so dry that little wildlife can live there. Birds such as terns, ospreys, pelicans and sea eagles nest on some of the islands, and depend on fish for their food. Some of the beaches also provide nesting grounds for turtles, such as the hawksbill, which swim to shore and dig holes in the sand to lay their eggs. When the little turtles hatch a few weeks later, they scuttle down the beach and return to the sea.

The Heart of the Muslim World

The Arabian Peninsula between the two seas is the home of the Arab people. It is also the centre of the Islamic religion, whose followers are called Muslims. This religion was founded in AD 622 by Muhammad, and his ideas and beliefs spread throughout Arabia and the Middle East. They were carried further afield by Arab traders into Africa, and east towards India.

Today, all the countries in the Middle East are Muslim, apart from Israel. Makka (Mecca), a town in Saudi Arabia not far from the Red Sea, was where Muhammad was born and is the most holy place in Islam. Muslims from all over the world try to make a **pilgrimage** to Makka at least once in their lives.

Thousands of Muslim pilgrims come to worship every year in Makka (Mecca), the most holy Islamic city. Makka lies on the Arabian Peninsula, not far from the Red Sea.

As Islamic religion spread round the region, it carried with it Arabic ways of life. Therefore, as well as being Muslim, most of the countries surrounding the Red Sea and Arabian Gulf have Arabic as their language and an Arabic culture.

Iran (once called Persia) differs from the other Muslim countries of the Middle East. The people are not Arab but Persian, and speak the Persian language. Long ago, there were disagreements over leadership in the Muslim world and Islam split into two main branches: the Sunnis and the Shi'ites. Whereas the majority of the world's Muslims are Sunni, those in Iran are Shi'ite. These two branches of Islam do not always see eye to eye and there are sometimes conflicts.

Along the southern borders of the Red Sea on the African side, the Arab races gradually give way to Africans. The people of southern Sudan and Ethiopia are mostly African and have their own languages. Many are Christians, not Muslims.

Above: In all but a few of the Muslim countries of the Middle East women are expected to cover themselves from head to foot so that no part of their body shows.

Right: Like this man from Yemen, many of the people living along the shores of the Red Sea and Gulf are Arabic.

Arabian sheikhs

There are seven countries in the Arabian Peninsula, the largest of which is Saudi Arabia. Those countries where oil has been found are extremely rich. The Gulf states (the Arab countries fronting the Arabian Gulf) are ruled by kings called sheikhs or emirs, who are the head of the controlling family. The royal families are very large: for example Ibn Saud, who founded Saudi Arabia in 1932, had forty-four sons by twenty-two wives. Today there are about 6,000 Saudi princes.

Traders and Sailors

For centuries, the Middle East was an important centre of trade because it lay on the route between East and West. Arabs controlled much of the business. Many goods were brought overland by camel train, but the Arabs were also great seafarers. As long as 2,000 years ago, they travelled in their wooden ships, called *dhows*, from the shores of the Red Sea and the Gulf to India, and even reached China. Their cargoes were mainly high-priced luxuries, such as spices, silks and jewels. Arab sailors also traded in ivory, amber, iron and slaves along the coasts of East Africa. Many set up businesses and settled in the countries they visited.

The Arab hold on trade became weaker from the sixteenth to eighteenth centuries. As their ships improved, Europeans started to sail direct to the Far East, avoiding the need for the markets of the Middle East. But when Europeans then began to **colonize** countries in the Indian Ocean, merchants used the Gulf as a trade route because it was the shortest way to take goods to and from Europe. Places such as Kuwait and Bahrain grew as staging and supply points.

Below: Once camels were used for taking goods across the deserts of the Middle East. Today these Bedouin offer camel rides to tourists who visit the Red Sea.

Above: **Dhows** *are still to be seen sailing along the coasts of the Gulf.*

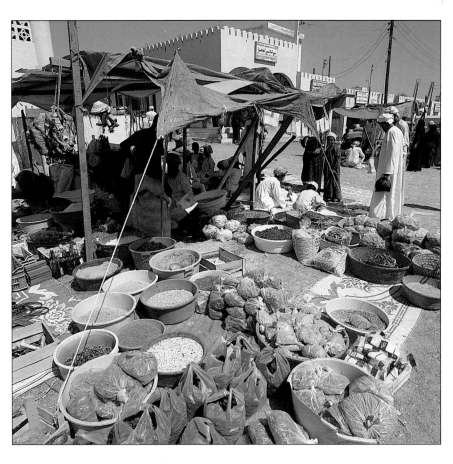

Pirates used to plunder ships passing through Gulf waters, and for a while, the southern coast of the Gulf was known as the Pirate Coast. The British signed **treaties** in the 1800s with many of the Gulf states to control piracy and protect British supply routes to India. These Gulf states have only become completely independent of Britain over the last thirty years.

The Arabs were some of the first traders to sail to the Far East and bring spices to the West. Spices are still sold in markets all over the Middle East.

Overland trade through the Middle East lost its importance in 1869 when the Suez Canal was completed. By linking the Red Sea with the Mediterranean, goods could be taken direct by ship between Europe and the Far East. Nowadays, although Arab *dhows* still sail along the coasts of Africa and India, most of the seaborne trade is the endless traffic of large tankers from the Gulf, which take oil all over the world.

Slaves

For hundreds of years, one of the main seagoing cargoes on these seas was African slaves. The Arabs were some of the first to deal in the slave trade. They took Africans from East Africa both for their own use and to supply European colonies in the area. At times during the 1800s, each year 10,000 slaves were being transported north to the Middle East and India. Even until the 1930s, wealthy Arab families kept African slaves to tend their livestock and to work in their households.

From Farming to Cities

As well as being great traders, the Arab people around these seas lived by fishing, growing dates and herding animals. Because of the lack of water for growing crops, many could only survive by keeping animals that could **forage** on desert **scrub**. Some people still follow the traditional ways of life, but the discovery of oil in the Gulf has meant that most people leave farming to go to cities where work is better-paid.

The Bedouin are the main group of Arabian desert herders. They live in small family groups keeping goats and sheep that graze rough grass and bushes found on the desert fringes. The Bedouin are traditionally a **nomadic** people, moving their tents from place to place in search of food for their animals.

Where there is enough water, the land is farmed. In desert **oases**, water from underground wells is used to grow wheat, vegetables and fruit, especially dates. The most productive farming areas are the Tigris, Euphrates and Nile river valleys, where it is also possible to grow rice, cotton and sugar cane, crops that need more water. By using **desalinated** sea water and modern **irrigation** systems, desert is being turned into new farmland near some cities on the Gulf coast.

Right: Modern, air-conditioned buildings sprout up in the heart of Bahrain, a rich island kingdom in the Arabian Gulf.

Dates grow at the top of tall palm trees, which makes them hard work to harvest.

Lifestyles have changed most in the countries where oil was discovered. Cities and ports were built with the money from oil and people moved there to work on oil rigs, on building sites, in factories and in offices. Today, about 90 per cent of people in the Gulf live in urban areas, many of which are on the coast. Places such as Bahrain and Kuwait are very modern, with towering skyscrapers and luxurious houses with air-conditioning and swimming pools. The main industries are oil processing, supplying oil rigs, carrying out ship repairs and cargo handling.

Foreign workers

During the 1970s and 1980s, millions of people, mostly from other Arab countries such as Egypt, Yemen and Jordan, arrived in the Arabian Gulf to work in the oil industry. In Qatar, for example, 90 per cent of the workforce is from abroad, and in Kuwait about half the population are outsiders. More recently, workers have been coming from Asian countries such as Pakistan, South Korea and the Philippines. There are tight restrictions on where immigrants can live and work and no outsider is allowed to stay permanently.

There are far fewer towns on the Red Sea. Jeddah is the largest, and, as well as being one of Saudi Arabia's biggest industrial ports, is the arrival point for the many thousands of Muslims who visit Makka (Mecca) each year. Aqaba, Port Sudan and Suez are important because they are the main Red Sea ports for Jordan, Sudan and Egypt.

Water

The key to life in this desert region is water. Where there is water, people can grow crops and build towns. In Egypt and Iraq, most people live in the large river valleys of the Nile, Tigris and Euphrates, where there is water all year round. Israel and Jordan share water from the River Jordan. Elsewhere, villages and small towns have grown up around wells, which draw on underground reserves of water, called **aquifers**.

Over the last fifty years, the population has been growing fast, and so has the need for water. In all Arab countries, the supply of water can now barely keep up with the demand. River and aquifer water is fast being used up and in some countries, water has to be piped from long distances away. It is likely that water supplies will run out before the oil, and water could become just as valuable. There are bound to be arguments over the right to use water, especially along rivers such as the Tigris and Euphrates, which run through different countries.

Building irrigation channels, such as this one in the United Arab Emirates, means that crops can be grown even in the desert.

A desalination plant in the United Arab Emirates. Here salt is removed from sea water to produce fresh water that can be used in homes, factories and farms.

The greatest demand for water is in the growing cities of the Gulf, where there are almost no natural, fresh-water supplies. As well as being used by households and industry, large amounts of water are being used for new irrigation projects to grow crops in the desert.

Sea water cannot be used because it is too salty, but it can be desalinated. This is a process that removes salt from sea water turning it into fresh water, but it uses a lot of fuel and so is very expensive. For the oil-rich countries of the Gulf, this is no problem, and some of the first and biggest desalination plants in the world were developed here. Countries such as the United Arab Emirates, Kuwait, Qatar and the state of Bahrain depend completely on desalination for their water.

Water from an aquifer reaches the surface in various ways.

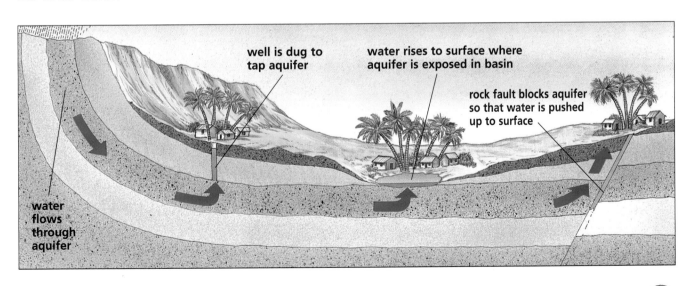

well is dug to tap aquifer

water rises to surface where aquifer is exposed in basin

rock fault blocks aquifer so that water is pushed up to surface

water flows through aquifer

Oil and Gas

The Arabian Gulf is the most important oil-producing area in the world. Oil is found both onshore and offshore under the sea-bed. The main producers in the Middle East are Saudi Arabia, Iran, Iraq, Kuwait and the United Arab Emirates. Between them, these countries have more than half of all the world's known oil reserves. They only use a small amount of the oil they produce themselves, so most of the oil is exported. The Gulf also has large reserves of natural gas.

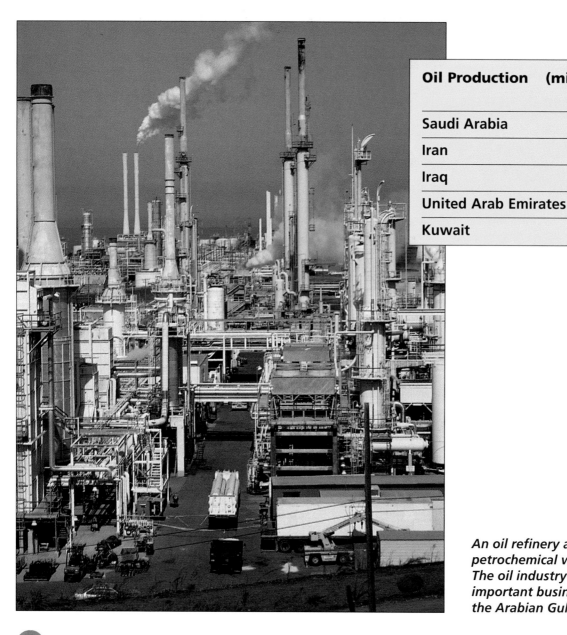

Oil Production	(million barrels per day)
Saudi Arabia	6.2
Iran	3.1
Iraq	2.1
United Arab Emirates	2.1
Kuwait	1.1

An oil refinery and petrochemical works in Dubai. The oil industry is the most important business for people of the Arabian Gulf.

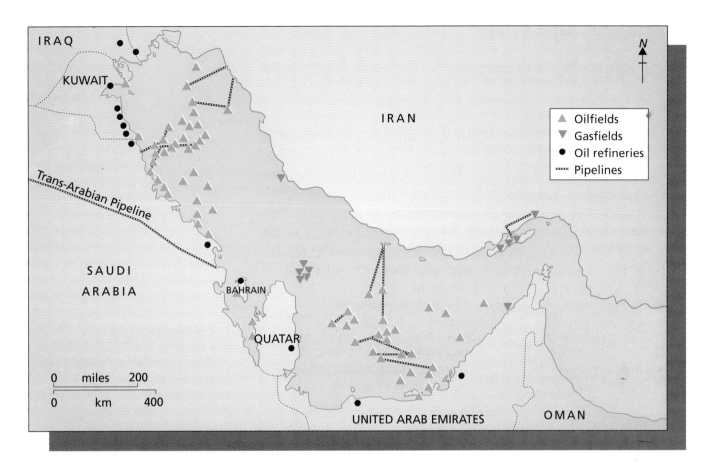

We could not live as we do without oil. The oil that comes straight out of the ground is called crude oil and for most uses it has to be **refined**. It is burnt as a fuel for heating houses and in power stations, and is refined into petrol and diesel as fuel for cars, trucks, planes and ships. Some oil is turned into paraffin and lubricating oil for machinery. It is also the raw material used to make chemicals, fertilizers, plastics and medicines. Natural gas is mostly used as a fuel.

Oil and gas are made naturally by **organic** matter **decomposing**. Over millions of years, organic sediments that collected in the basin of the Arabian Gulf were covered by sandy and muddy sediments which hardened into rock. Through heat and pressure of the rock above, chemical changes caused the organic sediments to turn into oil and gas.

Oil and gas can filter upwards through soft rock, but where they meet very hard rock they become trapped. Reservoirs of oil and gas collect under the rock; large reservoirs are known as oil or gasfields.

This map shows the huge number of oilfields in Gulf waters. There are also numerous oilfields and pipelines on the land and around the sea.

Oil Reserves	(Percentage of total world oil reserves)
Saudi Arabia	25.8
Iran	9.3
Iraq	10.0
United Arab Emirates	9.8
Kuwait	9.5

From Sea-bed to Shore

Expensive and highly technical equipment is needed to extract the oil from under the sea-bed, but the shallow and calm waters of the Gulf make it easier here than in many other seas. An oil rig consists of a metal platform, called the deck, supported on concrete or steel legs. These are drilled into the sea-bed to hold the rig in place. On the deck is the drilling equipment, as well as living accommodation for the oil-rig workers. The rig may be far out to sea, but people work here for weeks at a time and all supplies have to be brought out to them.

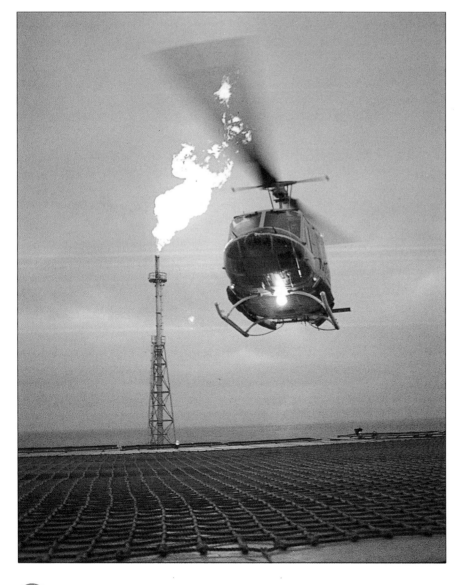

A helicopter brings workers to an oil rig out at sea. Behind the helicopter burns a flare of gas. Gas comes out of the ground with the oil and is often just burnt off.

Oil is extracted from the underground reservoir by long tubes (sometimes several kilometres long) which are let down through the water and drilled through the rock above the reservoir. The oil and gas are under pressure because they are squeezed by water and rocks. Once the reservoir is punctured, oil and gas pour out along the tubes to the rig above. As the reservoir empties, the pressure falls and water or gas is pumped back in to force out the oil.

Often a burning flare is seen above oil rigs, which is gas being burnt off. Gas is often wasted in this way if there is just a small amount in the reservoir, because gas is not as easy to collect as oil. On gas rigs, gas is collected, converted to a liquid and then transported in tankers, in a similar way to oil.

Oil is pumped to shore along pipes or collected by tankers, and taken to storage tanks or refineries. Most Gulf oil is exported as crude oil, but Gulf states refine some themselves. Oil is shipped around the world by tanker and across the Middle East by pipelines through the desert. Two long-distance pipelines are the Trans-Arabian Pipeline, which runs from Saudi Arabia to the shores of the Mediterranean (currently unused because of political problems), and the Sumed Pipeline, which carries oil from the Red Sea to the Mediterranean region.

Pipelines such as this one in Egypt run across the deserts of the Middle East, taking oil from storage tanks by the coast to towns and cities inland. Pipelines are a relatively simple and quick way to transport oil long distances overland.

Water Highways

Oil is the main cargo passing through Gulf waters and most is shipped to Europe, the USA, Canada and Japan. A large amount of oil traffic passes through the Red Sea as well because ships travel this way to reach the Suez Canal. A variety of goods come south through the canal – some of the biggest shipments are cereals from North America, fertilizers and machinery. The cargoes are not just for Middle Eastern countries, but also for Asian and even Australian ports far beyond.

The majority of ships are tankers and the largest, called supertankers, can carry about 500,000 tonnes of oil and are over 400 metres long. Navigating these ships can be difficult.

An oil tanker docks at a special quay built out into the sea in Kuwait. Pipes feed oil directly into the tanks in the holds of the ship.

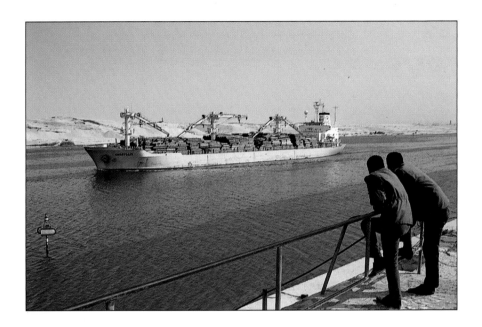

A cargo ship sails through the Suez Canal. The canal has been built through the desert to link the Mediterranean Sea with the Red Sea.

In the Red Sea the narrow channels are restricted by coral, and in the Gulf there is a lot of other traffic to avoid. The straits at the southern ends of both seas are narrow and shallow, and ships have to be carefully guided through.

The Suez Canal is an important short cut for international sea transport because it avoids the need for ships to take the long route round Africa. Without the canal, an empty tanker returning from north-west Europe to Saudi Arabia would take thirty-six days sailing round Africa, but it can do the journey in twenty-two days via the canal. The canal is basically a deep trench cut through the narrow neck of land between the Mediterranean and Red Sea. Sections of the canal pass through shallow lakes in which channels have been dredged.

Although oil traffic is still a large share of Suez Canal business, Middle Eastern oil exporters use the canal less than they once did. The Six-Day War in 1967 closed the canal and producers found other ways of transporting oil. Supertankers were developed to carry oil cheaply in bulk, and oil pipelines were built. Even though the canal is now open again, and has been deepened and widened, many supertankers are too big to use the canal when they are fully laden. Pipelines such as the Sumed Pipeline which is already carrying twice the amount of oil passing through canal, are likely to take more oil in the future.

The Suez Canal	
Opened	1869
Length	163 km
Width	Varies, but some sections are not wide enough for two ships to pass through.
Depth	17 m
Average travel time	15 hours
Red Sea Terminus	Suez
Mediterranean Terminus	Port Said

Harvest of the Seas

Fish are an important part of the diet for people who live along desert coasts. Many kinds of fish are caught in the Red Sea and Gulf, from little fish, such as sardines and snappers, to larger sharks and barracudas. The seagrass beds in the shallow waters of the Gulf are particularly rich in shrimps.

Yemeni fishermen bring in their catch on the beach. There is a rich variety of fish in both the Red Sea and the Gulf of Aden and the Yemen has a growing fishing industry.

Some fishermen still use their traditional boats to catch small amounts of fish for food or to sell at local markets. There is more small-scale traditional fishing in the Red Sea than in the Gulf. People in the Gulf have become less dependent on fishing for their livelihoods since the discovery of oil, and fishing has become **commercialized**. Fleets of motor trawlers bring fish and shrimps into ports at Bahrain, Kuwait and Qatar. Because of the heat, most ships are refrigerated to keep the fish fresh until it is brought to shore.

Fish stocks are falling in the northern part of the Arabian Gulf because dams on the Tigris and Euphrates rivers are stopping nutrients, upon which so much sea life depends, from entering the sea. Pollution of the water from oil spills is also taking its toll on fish catches, particularly the important shrimp industry.

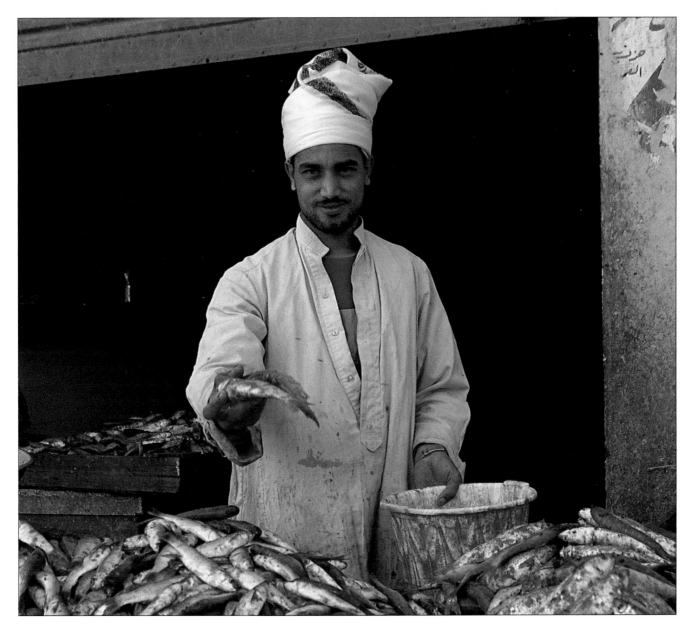

One of the oldest industries in the Gulf is pearl fishing. Pearls are found in oysters and are worn as jewellery. For hundreds of years, good quality pearls were harvested from oysters in sandy, shallow bays in the Gulf. Bahrain was one of the main pearling centres. At one time as many as 40,000 people from all over the Arabian Peninsula were employed in pearling. Divers would swim underwater for minutes at a time, holding their breath while they filled baskets with oysters. During the 1930s, the Japanese found a way of farming oysters to produce pearls, known as cultured pearls, which were much easier to harvest. The oil business also attracted people away from pearling in the Gulf, and as a result, pearling has now almost died out in the region.

An Egyptian fishmonger. A lot of the fishing in the Red Sea is still just for local markets and done on a small scale in the traditional way.

Old Resources, New Resources

Before the discovery of oil, salt was one of the most valuable minerals found in the Gulf. In the past, salt was used to help preserve food and it still is an essential part of our diet. Along the shallow Arabian coasts of the Gulf, there are large areas of natural salt flats, called *sebkhas*, where the hot sun has evaporated the sea water. Mixed with mud and sand, the salt lies as a thick crust up to 1 m thick. For hundreds of years, blocks of salt were dug up and taken by camel inland to market. Although the salt industry is now less important, salt is still extracted from the *sebkhas*.

Relatively little oil has been found in the Red Sea, but scientists have discovered another mineral resource which might be used in the future. Below the hot, salty water in the

One of the largest Red Sea holiday resorts is here at Eilat, in Israel, in the Gulf of Aqaba.

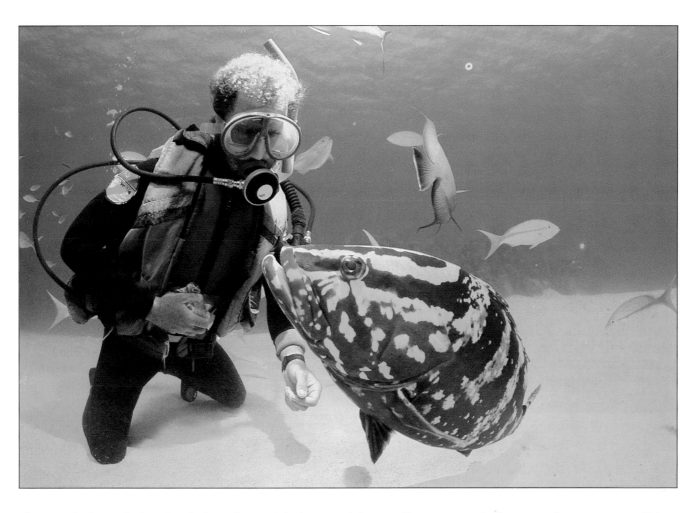

deep clefts of the Red Sea is a thick, muddy sediment containing large quantities of valuable metals such as iron, zinc and copper. The minerals lie so deep that no one has yet found an easy way to extract them, but it may be possible to pump up the muddy sediment to a ship and then extract the minerals.

It is only in recent years that tourists have started to appreciate the lovely coral reefs and the clear, warm waters of the Red Sea. The fantastic variety of sea life is a spectacular sight. Many tourists, especially divers, visit the Red Sea every year, but there are still relatively few resorts, mostly along the Egyptian coast. The beauty and interest of the reefs could attract more tourists and money to the poorer countries in the area, such as Sudan, but careful control is needed to preserve the reefs and their wildlife. There are fears that too many tourists would disturb fish and that pollution from big tourist developments might kill coral and other sea creatures. Egypt has already set up marine conservation areas where diving is controlled.

A diver watches a grouper fish. The clear waters and wonderful sea life make the Red Sea one of the most popular places in the world for diving.

Rich Seas, Troubled Seas

The discovery of oil has brought greater changes to the region than anything else in the last few hundred years. Some countries have become fabulously wealthy – Saudi Arabia and Kuwait are now two of the richest countries in the world. The money has enabled them to build houses, factories and roads and provide good welfare services such as schools and hospitals for their people. They can also afford to provide fresh water, both for cities and new farms in the desert, using the expensive desalination process.

Other Muslim countries around have benefited as well. Thousands of people have jobs working in the oil business and the richer states have helped poorer Muslim neighbours by giving them money for new projects.

Even though the oil has brought wealth, it has also brought trouble. There have been several disputes over ownership of the oil-rich territories, such as Iraq's invasion of Kuwait in 1990. The invasion became a major world incident because of international worries about protecting future oil supplies. Thousands of people were killed in fighting and there was

Above: An oil well burns in Kuwait at the end of the Gulf War, belching black smoke and blotting out the sun. It was several months before all the fires were put out.

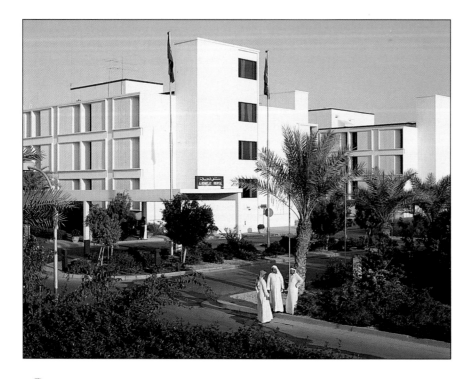

Oil has brought great wealth to countries such as Saudi Arabia which have been able to build modern hospitals such as this one for their people.

massive oil pollution in the Arabian Gulf when oil wells were destroyed or set on fire. Clouds of black smoke filled the air and oil leaked out across land and water, contaminating desalination plants and poisoning wildlife in the sea.

The vast amounts of oil being extracted and transported around the Red Sea and Arabian Gulf pose great dangers to the environment of the seas. The risks are greater than in an open ocean because the seas are virtually enclosed and it could take a long time for pollution to be washed away (although the warm water and sunshine in the area are a help in breaking down oil pollution). Oil spills occur regularly despite controls over safety on oil tankers, rigs and pipelines. However, there is concern for the environment in this area and regional action plans have been set up to watch over the two seas. There is hope that pollution can be controlled so that the rich, varied natural life in the Red Sea and Arabian Gulf will not be harmed as it has in some seas of the world.

Despite the huge amount of shipping traffic that passes through the waters of the Red Sea and Arabian Gulf, these seas remain some of the cleanest and most unspoilt in the world.

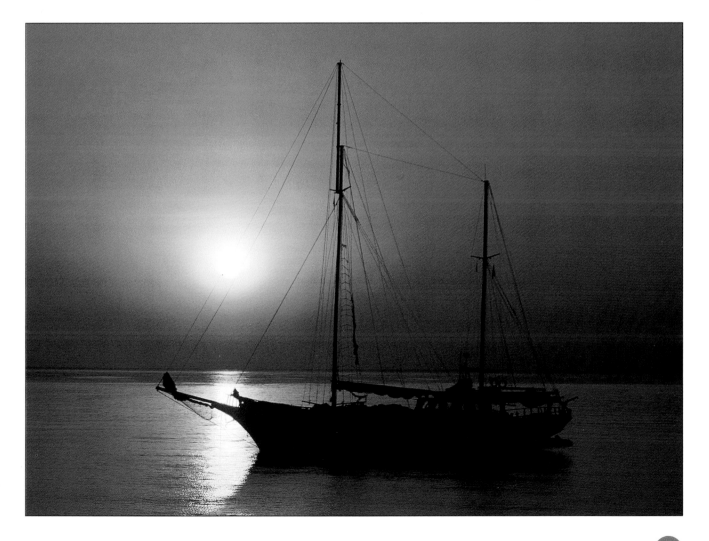

Glossary

algae Simple water plants, ranging in size from microscopic phytoplankton to giant seaweed.

aquifers Rocks that contain water within their pores or joints. They form underground reservoirs of water that can be reached by wells.

barrier reefs Coral reefs found further out to sea in deeper water. They are usually separated from the shore by wide lagoons.

colonize To conquer, settle in and control another country.

commercialized Used to make a profit.

continent A large area of land such as Africa.

decomposing Decaying.

delta A flat, fan-shaped area of land where the mouth of a river approaches the sea.

desalinated A process by which salt is removed from sea water so that it can be used as fresh water.

dredged When a canal, river or other waterway is deepened.

evaporates When a liquid, such as water, heats up and changes into a vapour.

forage To search around for food to eat.

fringing reefs Coral reefs lying close to the shore.

geological history The history of how the earth and its rocks have developed.

habitat A particular type of place where plants and creatures live.

irrigation Using channels or pipes to water the land.

isthmus A narrow piece of land connecting two larger pieces of land.

lagoons Areas of sea water, rather like lakes, separated from the open sea by sandbanks or reefs.

landlocked Completely, or almost completely surrounded by land.

navigate To find a safe route for a ship.

nomadic A type of lifestyle that involves moving from place to place to find food and water.

nutrients Basic substances such as minerals that are dissolved in water.

oases Fertile patches in deserts.

oil reserves Underground reservoirs of oil that have not yet been tapped or exploited.

organic Describes something that comes from an animal or plant. Organic sediments are small particles made up of the dead remains of plants and creatures.

peninsula An area of land mainly surrounded by sea but joined to a larger area of land.

pilgrimage A journey to a holy place.

predators Animals that hunt and kill other creatures for food.

refined Processed to get rid of impurities.

scrub Bushes and small trees.

seasonal Something that happens only at certain times, or seasons, of the year.

sediment Fine particles of rock and earth, such as mud and sand.

silt Very fine mud or clay that is carried along by a river.

squalls Sudden, strong winds or brief, violent storms.

strait A narrow sea channel that has formed between two areas of land.

subsistence Making a living that only provides the basic necessities of life such as food and water.

tankers Large ships that can carry liquid cargoes.

tidal range The difference between the height of the water at low and high tide.

treaties Formal agreements between countries.

Further Information

There are very few books about the Red Sea and Arabian Gulf, so look out for general books about seas and oceans and countries of the Middle East.

FOR YOUNGER READERS:

Ganeri, Anita, *The Oceans Atlas* (Dorling Kindersley, 1994)
Mason, A., *People and Places: Middle East* (Macmillan, 1988)
Morrison, Ian A., *World in View: The Middle East* (Heinemann, 1990)
Waterlow, Julia, *Deserts* (Habitats series) (Wayland, 1995)

FOR OLDER READERS:

Doubilet, D. and Ghisotti, A., *The Red Sea* (Swan Hill Press, 1994)
Elder, D. and Pernetta, J., editors, *Oceans* (Mitchell Beazley, 1991)
Pernetta, John, *Philip's Atlas of the Oceans* (Reed International, 1994)
Stevenson, R.E. and Talbot, F.H., editors, *Oceans* (Time-Life, 1993)
'The Desert Sea', *National Geographic* Vol.184, No.5, November 1993

USEFUL ADDRESSES:

Greenpeace
30–31 Islington Stret
London N1 7JQ

The following organization produces up-to-date briefings and education packs for students on a variety of world issues.

Understanding Global Issues
European Schoolbooks Publishing Limited
The Runnings
Cheltenham GL51 9PQ

Index